THE

NOT
OVERTHINKING

BELIEVING IN YOURSELF AND BUILDING YOUR DREAM LIFE

SHAURYA KAPOOR

Made with ♥ on the Notion Press Platform
www.notionpress.com

To every soul

who overthinks & feels misunderstood.

Contents

CHAPTER I

You Deserve Love

If you're hurting today, know that this feeling is only temporary, like all your other feelings. If happiness could leave your heart so unexpectedly, this helplessness and pain will also leave soon. You don't need to be hard on yourself every day just because life is difficult. Just because you're carrying mountains on your shoulders does not mean there's no happiness left in your story. Life is about trusting the universe, God, or whoever you believe in, especially yourself, and holding on to hope even on days when all you want to do is quit. You've come so far with a smile on your face and the kind of courage that can make warriors jealous. Don't give up, okay?

Notice when you overthink the most. Is it when you're by yourself in your room? Is it even when you're surrounded by people? Is it at night before you go to bed? No matter who tells you what, you're not a victim. You're not at the receiving end of something over which you've no control. You get to control your mind. Whenever you notice negative thoughts crippling in your head, distract yourself. Go for a walk. Talk to a friend. Start watching a show. Divert your focus entirely from those thoughts. It doesn't mean you're running away from your thoughts. It simply means you're choosing not to engage with negativity. You're choosing to focus on things that give you happiness instead of letting your negative thoughts consume you entirely.

When you're overthinking, start questioning yourself about why you are thinking that way. If your anxiety tells you you're going to fail the test, remind yourself that there's no way to find out what happens except waiting for the results patiently. And even if you fail, it won't mean the world has ended. I'm not saying your fears aren't real; all I'm saying is that you're making yourself sad about things that may never happen by making up scenarios in your head. Stop hurting yourself like that. If there's pain in the future, let it be in the future. Overthinking complicates everything and simplifies nothing. You're allowing your anxiety to steal your smile when you can simply trust your journey, hard work, good heart, and intentions and walk ahead with perseverance and courage.

When you're overthinking, call someone who loves you enough to not judge you for your thoughts and feelings. Someone who doesn't invalidate your feelings. Someone who makes you feel understood and not unheard. Someone who doesn't make you feel guilty about feeling too much. Someone who will listen to you patiently. That could even be a therapist. Seek support when it's required. Don't be afraid of opening up to new people and experiences. Sometimes, some conversations help you way more than you can imagine. Some people understand your heart better than you. There are people out there who care about you so much, you've no idea. You don't need to thrive or struggle in isolation. It's okay to let your loved ones know that you need love. Call your favourite person up, okay?

Write your feelings down without lying to yourself. Your heart feels lighter when you write about what's making it feel heavy. Did someone hurt you? What exactly did they do to hurt you? How does it make you feel? Write it all down. Even if it doesn't fix the problem, you'll undoubtedly feel better. I know sometimes there's nobody to pour your heart into. Sometimes, you're struggling, and nobody even knows you're going through all of it alone. Sometimes, you're in pain, and the only person around is you. On days when there's nobody to hold you until you feel better, resort to writing about your feelings. Nobody has to read them. It's a way of letting it all out of your system so you don't feel so heavy anymore.

You're so amazing, but you keep forgetting that amazing people deserve amazing things, not anxious thoughts and a heavy heart. You deserve to carry so much joy within yourself that you can feel your heart overflowing. You deserve the best pancakes in the world, coffee that tastes like heaven, friends who support you at all times, a family that understands what unconditional love means and practices it every day, unending hope in your soul, fresh flower bouquets, someone to hold you on days when life gets complicated, soothing sunsets, and rainkissed afternoons. You deserve so much more than your anxiety is convincing you to believe. You deserve the kind of happiness that makes you wonder if it's all really happening - if your life is, in fact, synonymous with the word happiness.

I don't think your expectations were the problem. You do so much for the people you love, and therefore, you expect things from them too. And that's completely okay. You're not supposed to keep giving and giving and giving without receiving even an ounce of affection from someone. And no, you're not asking for too much. You're barely even asking for the bare minimum. Love, support, care, affection, and respect aren't things you need to be yearning for. People will gaslight you into believing that you need to lower your expectations. They'll tell you you're the problem because you don't love them "unconditionally." Why must you love someone unconditionally when they don't feel the same way about you? When they don't want to love you unconditionally, too?

You deserve joy even if someone you loved a lot stole all of it away and left without giving you closure.

You deserve peace even if you've grown up in a house that could never be your home. You deserve sanity even if the world around you is determined to drive you crazy. You deserve calm even if people keep trying to put you through storms. You deserve to be loved for who you are, even if the people around you have convinced you to believe you don't deserve to be loved. You deserve to laugh until your stomach hurts, even if people have hurt you in the past. Don't forget that you deserve all the great things in the world just because the people around you have failed to give them to you. Life can't always suck. Things can't always go downhill. Your worth will be seen by the right people at the right time. And life will give up on the idea of hurting you, too.

People can choose not to believe in your dreams. They can choose to push you down and hurt you, and that's not a problem. People are seldom okay with seeing other people grow. The problem begins when you start subscribing to their ideas and thoughts. When you start believing that just because they don't believe in you, you shouldn't believe in yourself either. That just because they think you're bound to fail, you will fail. Stop believing that someone else gets to decide how far you're destined to go. The problem is not other people's lack of belief in you but the fact that you're convinced they're right. They couldn't be more wrong, okay? You can achieve anything you want to in life. You can reach anywhere you intend to reach. You can be whoever you aim to be.

And if nobody has told you this yet, hear it from me: I believe in you. You're worth it.

There are moments when all we need is someone to listen to us.

Sometimes, all you crave for is someone to whom you can pour your heart out without thinking twice—without the fear of judgment. Someone who doesn't judge your emotional state. Someone who doesn't question or invalidate your feelings. Someone willing to provide you with comfort beyond logic and reasoning. Someone who understands how to be there. How to stay with someone who's hurting until they feel better.

There are people who care about you enough to listen to you without judging you or trying to convince you of the "correct" course of action. They know at that moment that you don't need advice, you just need someone to vent to. They are your people, so keep them close, always.

You had to go through the pain to become this relentless soldier even pain is scared of.

You deserve to binge-watch cute cat videos on the internet, put on a cosy hoodie and read a book in peace. Rewatch your favourite show and listen to the birds sitting on your windowsill singing sweet songs. Take an afternoon nap with nary a care in the world. Set the AC temperature the way you like it. Order your favourite food and explore new movies. You deserve to be easy on yourself on days when life gets overwhelming. You must choose to be kind, gentle, and nice to yourself on days when it's extremely difficult to do so. It's okay to stop and smell the roses. It's okay to relax for a while to rejuvenate. You don't have to lose yourself in a productivity race just because everyone else is doing it. In case nobody has told you this lately— you don't have to keep struggling at the expense of your sanity.

People's love for you can be inconsistent, but your love and respect for yourself cannot be.

There are days when you hurt yourself more than anyone else ever can. You say the worst things to yourself without thinking twice. You bully yourself. You question all your achievements. You make yourself feel so small; it's concerning. If you value yourself only when you're shining bright —when everything's working out for you, and life is going great, you don't value yourself at all. You value your achievements. Worldly accomplishments. It's not you whom you care about; it's what you're doing and achieving. If this is the case, you're no different from your toxic ex, who loved you only when it was convenient. You need to love yourself even at your worst. On days when nothing is working out for you, and you're failing. On days when life is a complete mess and the world is pushing you away. On days when hope is a distant dream and holding yourself together becomes difficult. Dare to love yourself when it's difficult. Dare to show kindness towards yourself when it doesn't come easily to you.

It's okay to let someone go when you're trying to be kinder to yourself. Someone who always makes you feel bad about yourself. Someone who insults you in front of other people and then calls it a "joke." Someone who doesn't respect you enough to believe in your dreams. Someone who mocks your dreams. Someone who feels great by making you feel horrible. So many people are a part of your life, but not many deserve to stay in your life. There are people who treat you terribly, and you still put up with their behaviour because you don't want to let them go. You're hurting yourself, and they're hurting you, too. If you love yourself, please don't surround yourself with toxic people. People who cannot respect you and are determined to make you feel terrible will continue to do so until you chuck them out of your life. This is your sign to do it. Right now. *Terrible days become good days when you get rid of terrible people.*

Sometimes, you overthink because of the things that have happened to you in the past. If someone you loved broke your heart, you question the intentions of everyone who comes next. Any person who shows interest in you is pushed away by you. You don't trust people easily anymore. You find it harder to open up to people. It's difficult for you to talk to people about your feelings. In case you can relate to this, please remember that not everyone is going to shatter your heart. Not everyone will ridicule your feelings. Not everyone will walk away from your life easily. Don't close your heart to people only because of the actions of one inconsiderate person. Part of loving yourself is also acknowledging that you're someone who deserves boundless love, and being open to receiving it. It's okay to take some time to trust someone or get into a relationship with them, but it's not okay to entirely give up on the idea of love because of someone who caused the kind of damage you had never imagined. You deserve to be loved, and you should never tell yourself otherwise.

If you feel like taking a break, allow yourself to take one. If you feel like going on a trip, don't think twice. If you feel like calling a friend to tell them you miss them, do it immediately. Don't overthink about things that don't deserve second thoughts. You're not a war zone. Your life isn't a battle. Not everything has to be carefully planned and executed. It's okay to be impulsive. It's okay to let your heart guide your actions sometimes. Feel your feelings completely in order to completely understand yourself and learn what exactly your heart craves for. Take the decisions that give peace to your heart and soothe your soul.

Consistent happiness comes with consistent self-love.

When good things finally start happening in your life, I hope you'll do better than thinking about what will happen if it all ends. I hope you'll embrace them with open arms and remind yourself that you deserve way more than that. You deserve the kind of happiness you've not even dreamed of having—the kind of joy that will astonish even you. Don't think about the worst outcomes possible. Expect the best, and don't settle for anything less, okay?

Remember, back in school, when the teacher used to make stars and smileys in your notebooks when your handwriting would be nice? Remember how happy that used to make you? You need to rediscover joy in the small things in life. You need to relish small achievements. Little victories mean a lot, trust me. Celebrate yourself for the things you conveniently forget to clap for. You completed an assignment on time and submitted it, be proud of yourself. You didn't mess anything up the entire week at work, be proud of yourself. You made a special meal for your parents, be proud of yourself. You took time out to reconnect with a friend you were losing touch with, be proud of yourself. Nobody gets to decide what's inconsequential in your life and what matters. If something puts a smile on your face, it is worth celebrating and cherishing.

I hope you stop expecting yourself to be perfect all the time. I hope you don't criticise yourself too much when things go wrong and remind yourself that you're only human and it's okay to fall apart sometimes. I hope you don't stop yourself from being vulnerable because you always expect too much from yourself. I hope you don't lose sleep over situations you had no control over. I hope you don't sacrifice your peace over things you did not see coming. The truth is, you're imperfect, and so is everyone else. That's what connects us all to each other. We're allowed to mess up. We're allowed to be heartbroken. We're allowed to shatter at times. Please don't be cruel to yourself. Promise me you'll be kinder to yourself.

You can spend a lifetime knocking on doors that are determined not to open, and it won't change anything. Stop trying to build space for yourself in the hearts of people who are living happily without you. Try to find happiness outside of them. You're overthinking day in and day out because of someone who didn't even think twice before hurting you. You're breaking yourself because of someone whose love for you was a smoke break—a mere pastime. You don't need to cry over people who won't bother wiping your tears. You don't need to overthink because of someone who isn't thoughtful at all. Stop spending your life chasing after people who you need to let go of.

One day, you will look back, and a smile will cover your face. You'll realise how strong you've been all along.

CHAPTER II

You Deserve Happiness

When someone breaks up with you and says, 'You deserve better,' it hurts until you accept that you genuinely do.

You were earnest and honest about your love to a concerning extent. You thought they would change, but they never did. They kept breaking your heart and triggering your insecurities. They made you insecure about things you were never insecure about. They made you cry for hours and then made you feel bad for feeling bad. When someone tells you that you deserve better, know it's their conscience talking. They know what they've done to you, and you're blind to all the damage.

People won't help you unless you're in a position of power. People won't support you in the beginning but will be there to take credit when you finally make it. People will judge you for dreaming too big only to go around telling everyone how much they helped you to achieve your goals later on. You're overthinking because people aren't displaying faith in your dreams, when in reality, their faith is of little consequence. They will tell you that you're the best person in the world once you prove them wrong. They will support you when you don't need their support. There are people out there who believe in your dreams because they believe in your potential. Listen to them and ignore the voices of others. Someone who isn't making a contribution to your success doesn't get to make comments on it either.

Things your loved ones may have forgotten to tell you, so let me:

- It's okay if you were in love with the wrong person. They taught you that your love isn't for everyone. Your energy is priceless, and your heart is precious.

- Just because things didn't work out in the past doesn't mean you don't deserve to dream as wildly as you want to.

- Friends who betrayed you were people who simply didn't know how to value your genuine friendship. It's not about you. You didn't deserve that betrayal.

- You're not the opinions of a toxic teacher or a problematic boss. Nobody gets to make you feel bad about yourself.

- You feel too much. You think too much. But you're not too much. The world needs you more than you think.

- People will hurt you, and sometimes they won't even be sorry about it. That's just life. Sometimes, people are trash, and you cannot do anything about it.

If you've grown up with a constant voice in your head telling you that you're not good enough, promise me you'll not spend your entire adulthood listening to that voice. Promise me you will choose to believe in yourself no matter how difficult it seems. Promise me you will be careful with your heart. Promise me you will never choose to hurt yourself. Promise me you will choose growth.

Promise me you will always feel enough, even if the world tries to convince you otherwise.

Toxic friendships will affect your self-esteem and make you overthink like no relationship ever can.

There are 'friends' who will mock you in public, crack jokes about your insecurities, and make you the laughing stock so that they look 'cool.' Please know that friends are supposed to make fun of you in private, and that too, to a certain limit. Your boundaries aren't meant to be overstepped. Friendship doesn't give someone a free pass to mistreat you—privately or publicly. There's a difference between someone who's a friend and someone who's keeping you around to make everyone laugh.

When you're overthinking about things going wrong, remind yourself that a shift in perspective is all it takes to feel better sometimes. What if it all works out in ways you didn't even imagine? What if your dreams translate into reality? What if you achieve everything you've wanted to achieve? Let your 'what ifs' be decorated with hope and self-belief. You don't need to constantly push yourself down because your own thoughts are constantly lying to you.

Things aren't as bad as they seem, and even if they are, remember that you're a good person, and beautiful things are always on their way to you, even if you can't see them coming yet.

People will not believe in you even when you try your best to convince them that your plan makes sense. They will doubt you at each step, but that doesn't matter. Their doubt in you and your potential shouldn't lead to self-doubt. You'll take a lifetime to recover from the regrets of believing those few negative opinions that stopped you from believing in yourself.

It's okay to tell people these things:

- Your words hurt me. Stop hurting me, or I'll have to ask you to leave my life. I still value you, but I can't keep you at the expense of my mental health.

- Friends aren't supposed to make you feel anxious, stressed, and insulted.

- You cannot talk to me like that. My love for you isn't your free pass to humiliating me.

- I've given you enough chances, and your behaviour has remained unchanged. I'm sorry, but I cannot associate with you any longer.

- There's a difference between jokes and mockery. You get to joke around with me, but you do not get to mock me.

- There are certain things I'm not comfortable discussing. Please do not cross my boundaries.

You can't just turn off your mind. It's difficult to overcome overthinking. But I think it helps to have the right kind of people in your corner. Someone to remind you that your thoughts are merely thoughts that sometimes have no connection to reality. Someone to remind you that you're a good person with pure intentions, and the universe will send you back the good energy that you consistently pour into the world. Someone to hold your hand and tell you that getting out of your head is a prerequisite to getting closer to peace. On some days, that someone has to be you.

You need to be there for yourself even when nobody else is around you.

The worst thing you can do to yourself is cling to a hope that's meant to betray you.

That person hurting you every day isn't capable of change, and even if they're, they're choosing not to change themselves for the better. That job where you feel demotivated every day isn't your dream job. You'll have to leave sooner or later. That toxic relative you keep giving second chances to consciously chooses to add to your pain. I believe people carry the potential for change, but I also believe that some people are just horrible people. They may be good to others, but they're horrible to you. It's a choice. A conscious choice they make every day is not to be kind to you, not put in efforts for you, and make you feel terrible. Clinging to fading glimmers of hope, expecting them to be better when you know they've not gotten any better despite the fact that you've voiced out how they're impacting you multiple times is a form of self-harm. Let them go.

Gratitude is so understated.

There are so many things and people you have in life whom you often end up taking for granted. You've so much in life that other people crave for but never achieve or receive. Despite the pain and problems, your life has people with rainbow hearts. You've accomplished so many goals over the years. You've grown so much as a person. Please be grateful for your blessings. Be grateful for how the universe has been working in your favour, even on days when you're cursing it. Be grateful for all the love that you've in your life. A life without gratitude is like the sun without light, the sky without stars, and the ocean without waves. You'll never be able to appreciate your life if you don't focus on the things that did work out in your favour.

Please don't isolate yourself in the face of a crisis.

When things go wrong, please don't think the ideal solution is to cut everyone off and become an island. When life stops making sense, you're not required to stop being friends with everyone. Healing happens when you're surrounded by love. The people you love will assist you in ways you didn't even imagine. Isolation waters overthinking. Isolation waters anxiety. Isolation seldom leads to introspection or translates to solitude. If you're going through something, please don't force yourself to disconnect from people who wish you well. The people whose hearts would break knowing you're keeping it all to yourself. Please open up to whoever you trust with your whole heart. They won't disappoint you.

I hope you never have to learn this the hard way, but someone who genuinely loves you won't ever be the cause of your overthinking.

You can't be anxious and in love at the same time. You can't constantly struggle and also consider that person your soulmate simultaneously. The person you choose to love should empower you, not leave you powerless. They should always make you feel understood, loved, heard, appreciated, and respected. Someone who's triggering your overthinking can never be someone who adds to your peace and calms your soul.

Be okay with disappointing people and being the villain in their story. It doesn't mean that you're a bad person; it simply means that they expected something of you that you didn't wish to be, and there's nothing wrong with that. Some people are impossible to please. They will never be happy with you, even if you bring mountains to their feet. You can make their pain your own, and they'll still end up adding to your pain. They'll try to guilt you into believing you're a bad person for not living up to their expectations, but that doesn't mean they're right. If you've given your best in a relationship, friendship or any bond, and you know your intentions have been pure all along, if you've tried to take into consideration their needs and desires and have always tried to practice kindness even on days when it was difficult, by letting them go, you're not losing anything at all. It's okay to let someone go if they're hampering your peace and are determined to take your efforts for granted while constantly demanding more from you.

Negative people trigger your overthinking. The people who yell and slam doors. The people who argue about the most trivial things and say hurtful things during arguments. The people who are inconsiderate about your feelings expect you to be okay with being mistreated. If you surround yourself with such people, you will never be surrounded by peace. Someone who constantly lets their anger get the best of them and is okay with hurting you over and over again deserves to be shown the door before they end up causing more damage than they already have.

Signs that you've started respecting yourself:

- You're okay with saying no to plans that involve people you do not wish to hang out with — people who make you feel terrible and are insensitive towards your feelings.

- You're okay with forgiving people but are very careful about who you allow to re-enter your life. You no longer treat yourself like a public park where people can enter and exit at convenience.

- You don't stutter while drawing boundaries. You don't let petty 'jokes' slide. You call people out when they hurt you.

- You don't overthink about why someone did what they did. You either have a conversation with them directly or choose not to give them your energy at all.

- You choose to engage in things that genuinely put a smile on your face. You don't engage in anything that drains you.

Your family can have your best interests at heart and still end up hurting you.

They can say things to you that can end up making you insecure about your appearance, aptitude, career path—anything and everything. When a close family member chooses to be unkind to you, please know it's okay to feel hurt. It's okay to have a conversation with them about it. It's okay to tell them it's not okay to hurt someone like that. Just because someone does a lot of good things for you doesn't mean they're allowed to mistreat you. Just because someone's older than you doesn't mean they're allowed to constantly make you feel horrible about yourself. It's okay to have a conversation about things that hurt you. Your home is supposed to be the place where your soul stays at peace. Your family is also capable of change, and people are imperfect. Don't think that you deserve pain just because the source of it is your home.

There are so many life experiences you've not hugged yet. So many sunsets waiting for your eyes. So many stories waiting to be told to you. So many people you're yet to meet and fall in love with. So many cafés dying to serve coffee to you. So many cuisines you're yet to try. So many books you'll accidentally end up discovering while walking in bookstores. So many songs you'll give your heart to. So many flowers you'll buy for yourself and also receive from your loved ones. So many journal entries you'll cherish in the future. So many birds you're yet to listen to sing. So many new fountain pens you're yet to try. So many rain-kissed afternoons you're yet to relish. There's so much more left for you to see beyond this temporary phase of pain.

Life gets easier when you give it some time. Please be patient, okay?

I don't think the 'right' people always stay. I don't think just because you decided to leave someone, you were the one who was 'wrong.' Please don't think it's okay for people you love to hurt you just because they claim to love you. Please be open to the idea of reminding yourself that you don't have to bear sleepless nights and an anxious heart only because someone refuses to fix their behaviour. Just because you thought someone was your soulmate doesn't mean you've to stay with them when they're clearly not treating you even with basic human decency, let alone the way you deserve to be treated.

CHAPTER III

You Deserve Peace

I'm sending love to you for choosing to be so brave when giving up would've been easier. I'm sending love to you for loving yourself through it all when siding with the world and belittling yourself would've been easier.

When you start trusting your potential, intentions, good work, and hard work, you eventually stop expecting the worst.

You stop wondering what would happen if nothing works out because you know you possess what it takes to build from scratch all over again. Overthinking gets controlled when your self-esteem is high, and your self-belief is higher. When you start trusting yourself more than you engage in negative self-talk, you heal parts of yourself that you didn't even know required healing.

Healthy love doesn't come with unhealthy patterns.

Healthy love doesn't come with hurtful comments during fights.

Healthy love doesn't come with sacrificing your self-respect.

Healthy love doesn't come with breaking every day and still not choosing to leave.

Healthy love doesn't come with compromising with your mental health.

I'm not proud of you if all you do is work. I'm not proud of you if you're reaching the peak of your career, but that's all you are doing. I'm not proud of you if you're sacrificing your sleep over work. I'm not proud of you if you've not done the things you love in a long time because you're too busy building your dream life while simultaneously breaking on the inside. I'm not proud of you if you're losing yourself to capitalism on a daily basis. I'm not proud of you if you've no time for your loved ones.

I'm not proud of you if you're working at the expense of your well-being and calling it 'growth'.

Sometimes, you need to remind yourself: I want to make myself happy, and if you're someone who cannot add to my happiness, I must subtract you from my life.

I do not deserve to be stuck in darkness when I very much deserve a bright life full of light. I do not intend to keep anyone in my life who is careless with their words and not careful with my heart.

You overthink because you care about people, and their actions impact you.

I'm not here to ask you to stop caring about people, but all I'm saying is, please start caring about yourself, too. You're not someone who deserves to feel this bad on a daily basis because of people's inconsistent behaviour. Yes, you love them. Yes, you care about them. But they do not seem to understand the gravity of the impact of their actions on you. They don't seem to care about how much they're hurting you on a daily basis. You're overanalysing everything they've said and done, and they're out there not even thinking about you. Stop hurting yourself like that.

You're so used to pleasing others that you forget you're trying to build a future that will impact you more than anyone else. People are a part of your life, but you're your life. You're supposed to live the life you create. You cannot be a passive receiver. When you're trying to shape your life as per the will of others, please remember that they're not going to be the ones dealing with the repercussions of the same. They won't even acknowledge that your life is the way it is because of them. They will take credit but never responsibility. Please don't build a life that isn't your dream life, only to please people who are impossible to please anyway.

You're complicating your life by overthinking about what might go wrong. Hear me out — you might fail. Things might not end up working out. The consequences of your actions may be ultimately the opposite of what you expected them to be. But despite it all, despite all the failures and heartbreak, you will somehow manage to move ahead bravely like you always have. You don't have a victim mindset. Even if things go wrong, you have it in you to make yourself feel better, and then everything will be all right again. Even if you lack the energy or courage to make things better, there are people you love who will be there to support you and help you build your dream life all over again. Don't be scared of taking chances because you think nothing is going to work out.

Please stop overthinking because of the opinions of other people.

There are so many people you dislike, sometimes even without having enough reasons to dislike them. There are so many people who annoy you, despite the fact that lots of people consider them amazing. Opinions don't matter until they come from someone who has been with you at your worst, holding your hand and guiding you through it all. Opinions don't matter until it's coming from a place of genuine concern. A lot of people will always have a lot of things to say about you no matter what you do in life, but what matters is how well you regulate your emotions and manage your self-esteem. Nobody's opinion matters as long as you believe in yourself.

If you're spending so much time overthinking about the things that might go wrong and are feeling anxious day in and out, imagine how much better your life will get once you start choosing your peace and happiness by expecting the best and reminding yourself that you deserve nothing but the best. Imagine how happy you will be when you stop letting your anxiety guide your mood and start believing that you're meant for beautiful things in life, and you deserve to smile a lot more and carry happiness in your heart at all times.

Do not lose yourself by constantly overthinking about things that might never even happen. You're missing out on the golden sunsets, brownies that taste like heaven, coffee with just the right amount of sugar, books that carry stories that will never leave you, and so much more, only because you're constantly punishing yourself by thinking negatively. Don't do that to yourself, okay? You deserve to be treated better than that by yourself. Especially by yourself.

It's an act of courage—choosing your own peace by letting go of negative thoughts that are determined to keep you at war with yourself.

What's meant for you isn't always what you think is meant for you.

The universe wants the absolute best for you, and sometimes that means removing people and things from your life that aren't supposed to help you grow and be happy in the long run. Learn to be okay with letting go of things and people when they show you they're only there to hurt you. Notice who makes you overthink more instead of overloving you. Notice who causes you more stress and reminds you of insecurities you had forgotten completely. Notice who reminds you of your trauma and remind yourself to detach yourself from them. You deserve happiness in its purest form, so let go if need be to find what you truly deserve.

Question your thoughts. If you're overthinking about potentially falling sick, visit a doctor and get a full body checkup done. If you're afraid about failing a test, write down the names of the chapters you've studied. If you're overthinking about whether or not a friend genuinely likes you, pick up the phone and call them immediately. If you're creating scenarios in your head that don't really exist in reality, know that you're putting yourself through pain that's really avoidable if you try to put everything in the context of reality and question your thoughts as they come instead of accepting them at face value and labelling them as the truth.

Please don't consume content that triggers your overthinking.

Choose to consume positive content because it's really easy to lose yourself in the ocean of millions of content pieces on the internet that are not necessarily good for your mind. When there's a lot of unnecessary information in your head, you're bound to overthink. Consume only what you want to attract in your life. Consume only what gives you peace and makes you feel better. Consume only what makes your heart feel lighter. Choosing to consume negative content is a form of self-harm.

Sometimes a deep breath is all it takes to feel better.

On days when you're feeling overly anxious, you'll notice how your heart starts racing and your head hurts too. You'll notice how you feel disconnected from reality and find yourself stuck in thoughts you can't even fully make sense of. On days like these, allow yourself to take a deep breath and relax for a while. Take as many deep breaths as you want until you feel better. Move. Go out and let the wind kiss you. Try to get yourself out of the negativity zone by taking deep breaths, closing your eyes, and allowing yourself to rejuvenate and exhilarate. It's the simple things that sometimes make all the difference.

Things will fall into place.

Your broken heart will heal. You won't feel this heavy all the time. Your eyes will carry happiness and not dark circles. You will sleep like a baby. You will start enjoying your favourite things again. You will laugh your heart out again to the point where your cheeks will turn pink like your favourite flowers. You will be so happy again that you'll forget about the pain of the past. The painful memories will stop resurfacing, too, after a while. All you need to do is be a little patient. Things fall into place when you give life some time.

You have it within you to build a beautiful life for yourself.

All you need to do is listen to that hopeful voice in your head that you always keep ignoring. All you need to do is follow your heart at times and let it take the lead. All you need to do is trust yourself and your own potential to achieve everything you want to in life. You deserve to create a gorgeous life for yourself, and I hope you come to realise that you have it in you to do the same, no matter who says what.

I hope you allow yourself to dream bigger than you're currently. I hope you believe that nothing is too good to be true for you. I hope you remind yourself of the beauty of your heart and the magnificent impact you cast on the people in your life. I hope you remember that hearts like yours are rare. Your depths remind me of the ocean, and I hope you don't settle for dreams that waves of negativity can perish. I hope you choose to build a life for yourself that's beyond your own expectations, and bigger than your own dreams.

The person who is meant for you will stay without loud fights and trauma.

They will stay without you having to run behind them to make them stay. They will stay without you having to constantly beg them to not treat you like shit. They will stay because leaving isn't an option they ever want to consider—because they know you do everything in your capacity to treat them the right way, and they want to treat you even better because they genuinely appreciate the love you carry in your heart for them. Wait for that person.

CHAPTER IV

You Deserve Healing

Sometimes, you don't get what you want, and I know it hurts, but you keep increasing the intensity of your pain by putting yourself down by saying terrible things to yourself—the kind of things you'd never say to someone you love. Listen to me—it's okay if the results did not match your expectations. It's okay if you thought something great would come out of something, and it didn't. I know you put a lot of hard work, time, and energy into it, and I know it's not easy to get over it, but the truth is, you're staying in the past despite knowing it has slipped away. You're punishing yourself every day for something that has already hurt you enough. Please don't break your own heart by reminding yourself of the things that went wrong in the past.

People will hurt you, but my love, why are you hurting yourself? Why are you being mean to yourself when you can practice kindness? Your little heart doesn't deserve the kind of pain you're giving it by disrespecting yourself.

Happiness isn't going to come to you until you come back to yourself and pour empathy, love, and compassion into your own heart.

People will tell you that you should focus on what the pain is teaching you instead of focusing on how it's making you feel. But sometimes, there's no lesson. And even if there is, you're too hurt to notice it. I want you to not overthink about finding a lesson in the pain and instead acknowledge that it's completely okay to feel broken sometimes. You're only human, and not everything has to be a moral science lecture. It's okay if you think some situations suck and you didn't deserve whatever happened. It's okay to process your feelings first and allow yourself some time to heal from things people want you to quickly recover from. Give yourself time to heal and learn to be okay with accepting that you're only human and no matter what anyone says, what hurts you, hurts you.

I don't want you to have regrets in the future—the kind that suffocate you on random days and don't let you sleep. Please don't give up on your dreams only because you're overthinking about everything and wondering what will happen if you fail.

Please don't sacrifice your dreams at the altar of fear.

Your idea of perfection is flawed.

You know what's really perfect? Going to sleep peacefully and content. Spending the entire day without feeling like you're carrying mountains on your back. Laughing like a baby and not having to fake your smile the way people do at work. Building a home that smells like love at all times. Surrounding yourself with people who genuinely care about you and want you to be happy. Perfection is living a life that makes you feel perfectly happy on most days. And even when sadness arrives, you've enough courage in you to know it's only temporary.

The older you get, the more you realise that the reason you overthink is because of the experiences that you've been through in the past. Sometimes, things continue to impact you even after you think you've gotten over them. Sometimes, your trauma manifests in ways you never expected it to. I hope you know that even the most gorgeous books have some bad chapters in them, and that's okay. It's okay if life failed you in the past because it won't always hurt you. Be hopeful and keep moving ahead, okay?

Notice who pays attention when you're talking about the things that matter to you. Notice who remembers them. Notice who consciously does things to bring a smile to your face. Notice who notices when you're upset and calms your overthinking. That is your person. Keep them close to your soul, always.

On days when life stops making sense, remind yourself that there are paintings in this world that you don't understand the meaning of until someone explains them to you. There are poems that are beautiful, but they don't make sense to you when you read them for the first time. There are so many things that don't make sense until they finally do, and that's when you realise the beauty they hold in them. Life has its own ways of unfolding in magical ways—ways you don't necessarily understand at first. Everything makes sense over time if you just give yourself enough time to process things and be patient through it all.

Gentle reminder: just because you put in a lot of hard work into something and it didn't work out doesn't mean it'll happen again. It doesn't mean you're a failure, and you should let your curiosity not reflect in your actions and become your reality. It doesn't mean you're bad at execution. It simply means that you're rare—not everyone has the courage to try new things and move ahead bravely when things don't work out. Not everyone has the courage to chase after their goals and never look back. Not everyone has the courage to believe in themselves enough to give new things a shot. You're not a failure. Stop being hard on yourself for no reason. Be proud of yourself for persevering, always.

Look at the past versions of you with more kindness than you currently do. You're the person you're today because of all the regrets, pain, trauma, empty promises, problematic relationships, and every experience that you've lived in life. Your past version didn't know any better than you did when you were in that situation, but that doesn't mean you don't need to look at it with kindness. It doesn't mean you're required to curse yourself for the mistakes that happened long ago. Be kind with all the versions of yourself that existed in the past and the version that exists in the present. Love is being gentle with your heart, in being kind to your soul.

It's okay if you're anxious right now. Your anxiety is probably because of everything that didn't go the way you expected it. Your anxiety is perhaps because of your relationship with someone or because of your relationship with yourself. Whatever you're feeling right now, I hope you know that it's not what you're made of. You're made of love, hope, gratitude, empathy, kindness, and compassion. You're made of stars and all the light in the world. This anxiety is not here to stay. It's a temporary visitor who needs to be shown the door as soon as possible. Don't make it feel welcome. Don't let it confuse you for its home. You're made of love and made to spread joy to the world and experience happiness in its purest form yourself. Don't let your anxious thoughts convince you to believe that you deserve to stay anxious all your life.

Sometimes, the bad place you need to get yourself out of is your own head. Sometimes, it's difficult to regulate your negative thoughts, and on those days, I hope you remind yourself of the power that rests within you. I hope you remind yourself that you've been strong all your life. You've dealt with so much by yourself, it's crazy! You've been through pain, heartbreak, loss, trauma, and endless nights full of anxiety. And you've made it out of all of it! You're a strong warrior, okay? Don't let your negative thoughts convince you to believe that you're not good enough or that you're not strong enough to deal with whatever has come your way. There's courage in you that's yet to be explored. Never forget that.

Learn to forgive yourself for the mistakes you've made in the past so that you can create a beautiful, heartwarming reality for yourself. It's okay to mess things up even after being confident you won't mess up. It's okay to not be the best at something you thought nobody could be better at than you. It's okay if things aren't going according to the plan you had in mind. Take a deep breath and let it all go. You don't deserve this heaviness you're carrying on your shoulders. Let it go. It doesn't deserve to remain a part of you.

You've so much time to do the things that make you stop overthinking. Spend time doing the things that make you feel lighter. Trying a new recipe. Working out. Going out for a walk. Talking to a friend. Sleeping in your mother's lap. Writing your thoughts down in a journal. Watching a movie that always makes you smile. Watching your favourite show again. Reading a new book. Exploring a new genre of music. Doing touristy things in a city you've lived in all your life. Do whatever it takes to make your little heart feel even a little better. Do whatever it takes to have new experiences and feel new feelings, okay?

It's okay to have lunch alone in the cafeteria. It's okay to take the bus back home because you can't afford a cab. It's okay to not be a part of the 'cool' group. It's okay to feel like a misfit. You don't have to force yourself to do things you don't want to do, only to be liked by people whom everyone likes, but in your heart of hearts, you've no idea why everyone likes them. Sometimes, you want to fit in so badly that you end up trying to change your entire personality only to be liked by people you don't even look up to. You're overthinking on a daily basis about why you're not a part of the 'cool' group when you need to remind yourself that you are the 'cool' group. You're the most fun person in the world, and the right people will love you for it. You don't have to turn yourself into someone you're not only to be liked by others.

Trying is better than sitting around all day overthinking about what might go wrong. I'm not here to tell you that everything will surely work out if you put in hard work. There are things that just don't work out, and you cannot do anything about it. But that doesn't mean you should give up on the idea of trying new things and implementing ideas you've been wanting to implement for a long time. That doesn't mean you need to live a life you're unhappy with because failing scares you more than unhappiness. Even if you fail, you'll still remain that one person with dreams in their eyes and courage in their bones. You'll always remain someone who has a lot of potential in them. You'll always remain someone I'll always root for and believe in.

Don't give up, okay? I love you.